Paper from Wood

by Emily Sohn and Pamela Wright

NORWOOD HOUSE PRESS
Chicago, Illinois

Norwood House Press
Chicago, Illinois

For information regarding Norwood House Press, please visit our website at www.norwoodhousepress.com or call 866-565-2900.

Contributor: Edward Rock, Project Content Consultant

Editor: Lauren Dupuis-Perez

Designer: Sara Radka

Fact Checker: Sam Rhodes

Photo Credits in this revised edition include: Getty Images: EyeEm, 12, hartcreations, 18, 16, 19, Westend61, cover, 1; Pixabay: GDJ, background, (tech pattern); Shutterstock: Maya Kruchankova, 4; Wikimedia: Jost Amman, 14, New York Public Library, 13, Unknown, 13

Library of Congress Cataloging-in-Publication Data

Names: Sohn, Emily, author. | Wright, Pamela, 1953- author. | Sohn, Emily. iScience.
Title: Paper from wood / by Emily Sohn and Pamela Wright.
Description: [2019 edition]. | Chicago, Illinois : Norwood House Press, [2019] | Series: iScience
  | Audience: K to grade 3. | Includes bibliographical references and index.
Identifiers: LCCN 2018057819 | ISBN 9781684509683 (hardcover) |
  ISBN 9781684043620 (pbk.) | ISBN 9781684043736 (ebook)
Subjects: LCSH: Paper—Juvenile literature. | Papermaking—Juvenile literature.
Classification: LCC TS1105.5 .S69 2019 | DDC 620.1/97—dc23
LC record available at https://lccn.loc.gov/2018057819

Hardcover ISBN: 978-1-68450-968-3
Paperback ISBN: 978-1-68404-362-0

Contents

Note to Caregivers:
In this updated and revised iScience series, each book poses many questions to the reader. Some are open ended and ask what the reader thinks. Discuss these questions with your child and guide him or her in thinking through the possible answers and outcomes. There are also questions posed which have a specific answer. Encourage your child to read through the text to determine the correct answer. Most importantly, throughout the book, encourage answers using critical thinking skills and imagination. In the back of the book you will find answers to these questions, along with additional resources to help support you as you share the book with your child.

Words that are **bolded** are defined in the glossary in the back of the book.

What's the Best Paper Product for a Dollhouse?

Do you remember the first time you held a crayon? As soon as you could draw, you used paper. In this book, you will learn where paper comes from and how it is made. You will also enter a contest. Then you'll decide which types of paper will be the best for making a paper dollhouse.

Paper House Contest

You've been asked to enter a contest.
You will make a paper house for paper dolls.
Houses will be judged by how strong they are
and how nice they look.

Which type of paper
will you use to make
the house? Here are
some choices.

Choice 1: Cardboard

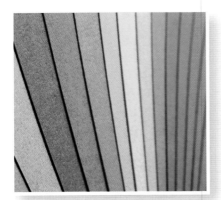

Choice 2: Construction Paper

Choice 3: Paper Towel

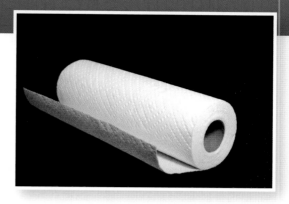

Choice 4: Writing Paper

Before you choose, think about these questions.

Which paper is strongest?

Which paper is easiest to shape?

Which paper is best to draw on?

Which paper is best to paint on?

Keep reading to learn more about paper. Use what you learn to make the best paper house.

Let It Rip!

Look around your home or school for paper.

See how many types you can find, besides the four dollhouse choices.

Make sure no one needs the papers anymore.

◆ Paper comes in all sorts of textures, colors, and thicknesses.

Now, rip them up!

Do some papers rip more easily than others?

Put the papers that rip easily in one pile.

How else are they alike?

How are they different from the other papers?

Find a magnifying lens or a microscope.

Use it to look at the ripped edges.

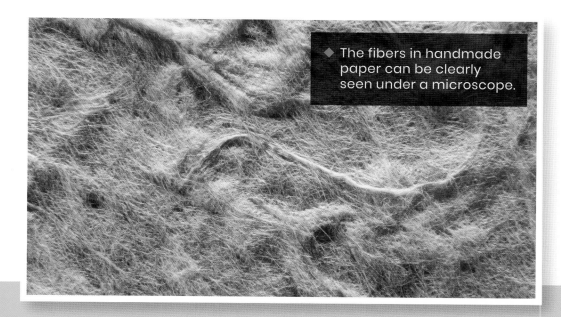

The fibers in handmade paper can be clearly seen under a microscope.

What do they look like?

Sort the papers by color.

Now, see which have similar thickness.

Which feel alike?

How else might you put paper into groups?

How Is Paper Made?

Before you start working on your paper house, let's learn how paper is made.

Paper doesn't grow on trees. But a lot of paper comes from trees. Trees have **fibers**. These fibers are called **cellulose**. These fibers are strong. They hold their shape well in water. Wood, which is mostly what trees are made of, has a lot of cellulose.

◆ Wood must be cut into small chips before it is made into paper.

So, how is paper made? First, workers strip **bark** from wood.

◆ stripping the bark

They cut the wood into chips about the size of nickels. The wood chips are made of fibers. Next, the workers mix the chips with water. This makes soft, wet **pulp.** The pulp is sprayed onto a big screen. The water drips away and the pulp starts to dry out. The fibers start sticking together.

◆ wood chips

◆ sheet of paper taken off screen

The pulp then goes through a machine that squeezes more water out. The fibers stick to each other even more. When the pulp is completely dry, paper is left.

◆ rolls of paper

◆ These trees could make a lot of paper!

Did You Know?

In the United States, about 70 million tons (63.5 billion kilograms) of paper and paperboard are used every year.

Using a lot of paper means we need a lot of trees! Good paper companies want to make paper and protect trees. They plant and grow new forests to replace the trees that have been cut down to make paper and other products.

Invention of the Printing Press

Around 1450, Johannes Gutenberg invented the printing press. The press used a set of movable metal letters and ink to print each page. It allowed people to make many copies of a book.

◆ Johannes Gutenberg

◆ Gutenberg Bible

Printers set the letters on a flat wooden plate. They put ink on the letters. Paper was placed on another wooden plate. Then they pressed the two plates together. This worked like a stamp. The printing press could print 250 pages an hour. Before this, copying a single book took a year!

◆ printer in 1568

Books became more common. More people began to read. The printing press helped spread ideas around the world.

◆ Handmade paper often looks very unique.

What Is Paper Like?

Our lives are full of paper. Some paper is thick, like the side of a box. Cardboard is used a lot to make boxes. Some is thin, like a page in this book, or writing paper. Some paper is soft, like tissues. Some is rough, like paper grocery bags.

You want to make your dollhouse as strong as you can. Do you think you should use thick paper or thin paper? Which of the four papers in the contest seem strong?

◆ Cutting paper changes its shape.

Shaping Your House

You want to win the contest. So your house needs to have a good shape. How will you form its shape? You can fold paper. You can cut it. What else can you do with paper to change its shape? How will you change your paper's shape to make your house?

Cutting Tricks

Now you know about fibers. That can help you build your house.

Here's a trick. Fold a piece of paper to make a **crease**.

◆ The folded edge is called a crease.

Now, fold it backward. This makes the crease deeper. You might see fibers start to break apart.

Hold a ruler against the crease. Tear the paper into two pieces. The edges are nice and straight. Who needs scissors?

Fold and cut thick paper. Now, fold and cut thin paper. Which is easier?

You can cut paper or tear paper for your dollhouse. Which would you rather do?

It's time to make your house look nice. Do you want to color or paint your house? Look at your paper choices. Take a sample of each type of paper.

◆ What type of paper is best?

First, draw on each of them with a crayon. Then color on them with paint and markers. Think about the questions below.

Which types of paper are good to write on?

Which types are good to color or paint on?

Do the paints or markers soak through some papers?

Is it easier to draw on smooth paper or rough paper?

Which kind of paper makes your art look best?

Paper Mill Worker

The paper products we use every day are made in a mill. Each type of paper has a special recipe. A worker mixes chemicals, water, and fibers into a machine. The machine creates different products. Paper towels, toilet paper, and drawing paper are all made in mills. Workers make sure each item is correct. Next, the worker sends the products to be packaged. They are then shipped to stores so people can buy them.

◆ Paper mill workers handle lots of paper every day.

Solve the iScience Puzzle

Are you ready to make your house? Here are your paper choices again. Each has good parts, called pros. Each also has some bad parts, called cons. How do you want your house to look and how strong should it be?

Type of Paper	Pros	Cons
◆ cardboard	Sturdy. Easy to paint on.	Too stiff to fold. Hard to cut.
◆ construction paper	Colorful.	Too dark to show some crayon or marker colors.
◆ paper towel	Easy to fold and cut.	Floppy. Tears easily. Hard to paint or color on.
◆ writing paper	Pretty strong. Good to draw and paint on.	May be too thin to last long.

Think about where your art projects go when you throw them out. One way to help trees is to use paper more than once. Find out if there is a **recycling** program in your town or city. See if you can get your school to use paper that has been recycled.

You can also ask an adult to help you learn how to make your own paper. You can learn how to do this in books or on the internet. Then you can use your own paper to write a book about paper!

Glossary

bark: the outer covering of the main part of a tree and its branches.

cellulose: a stringy substance; the main material in the cell walls of plants.

crease: a ridge created in something by folding it.

fibers: thin threads in a plant, tree, or paper.

pulp: a mix of water and very small chips of wood.

recycling: turning used materials into new things to prevent waste.

Further Reading

Noll, Tom. 2019. *The Flowerbed*. Recycling Creatively with L.T. Washington, DC: Green Kids Press.

Rodabaugh, Katrina. 2015. *The Paper Playhouse: Awesome Art Projects for Kids Using Paper, Boxes, and Books*. Gloucester, Mass.: Quarry Books.

Jackson, Demi. 2016. *How Is Paper Made?* Everyday Mysteries. New York: Gareth Stevens Pub.

How to Make Paper at Home: 13 Steps (with Pictures) - wikiHow. https://www.wikihow.com/Make-Paper-at-Home.

Additional Notes

The page references below provide answers to questions asked throughout the book. Questions whose answers will vary are not addressed.

Page 9: Paper can be sorted according to texture, strength, flexibility, or color.

Page 16: You can crumple it, roll it, and tear it.

Index